Alfred's Basic Piano Library

Prep Course

FOR THE YOUNG BEGINNER

Lesson Book • Level A

Willard A. Palmer • Morton Manus • Amanda Vick Lethco

Correlated materials to be used with *Prep Lesson Book, Level A:*

Title	Start on page
Prep ACTIVITY & EAR TRAINING BOOK, Level A	5
Prep FLASHCARDS, Levels A & B	8
Prep CHRISTMAS JOY, Level A	12
Prep NOTESPELLER, Level A	16
Prep SOLO BOOK, Level A	14
Prep TECHNIC BOOK, Level A	18
Prep THEORY BOOK, Level A	4

FOR TEACHERS ONLY: Teacher's Guide to Prep Lesson Book A

Illustrations by Christine Finn   Art Direction by Ted Engelbart   Production by Linda Lusk

A General MIDI disk (5700) and a Compact Disc (17159) are available, which include a full piano recording and background accompaniment.

 Alfred

Note to Parents and Teachers

ALFRED'S BASIC PIANO PREP BOOKS, Levels A and B, were written to answer the demand for a course of study designed especially for students who are five years and up.

These books take into consideration the normal attention span as well as the small-sized hands of the young beginner. The basics of music are introduced through the use of tuneful but simple music that advances at the proper speed for small children to comprehend and enjoy.

Each level contains a LESSON BOOK and a THEORY BOOK. After completion of the two levels, the student is ready to begin LEVEL 1B of the regular ALFRED'S BASIC PIANO LIBRARY.

It has been proven that students who begin at an early age develop faster and more easily in ear training, finger technic, and in musicality than those who begin later. Just as children grasp languages more rapidly than adults who study a foreign language, they also seem to grasp certain elements of musical language more easily than most later beginners. Almost all of the great musical geniuses, such as Mozart, Beethoven, Mendelssohn and Chopin, were playing well by the age of five.

Music is a language understood by people of all nations. It is one of the most basic mediums of communication and expression. Improved coordination, a broadening of interests, a discovery of the importance of self-discipline, the pride of achievement, and a world of pleasure are only a few of the rewards pupils receive from the study of music.

We offer our best wishes to you and your child or student in this new adventure. It is certain to be richly rewarding!

THE PUBLISHERS

Outline of Basic Concepts in Prep Book A

Pages 4–5   Introduction to playing.

Pages 6–15   BLACK KEYS used for keyboard orientation and finger number recognition, avoiding the association of any finger number with any specific key. Elementary rhythmic reading and development of finger skills. Introduction of basic dynamic signs.

Pages 16–17   Introduction to the identification of white keys in relation to black keys.

Pages 18–25   MIDDLE C POSITION. Fluent recognition of key-names through letter notes that move up or down on the page as if they were on the staff. This visual concept will lead smoothly into staff notations.

Pages 26–30   C POSITION in both hands. Tuneful pieces introduce new rhythmic patterns and build technical skills.

Pages 31–35   BASS STAFF. Pieces for left hand alone in bass clef. Letter-notes in bass clef gradually phased out.

Pages 36–39   TREBLE STAFF. Pieces for right hand alone in treble clef. Letter-notes in treble clef gradually phased out.

Pages 40–47   GRAND STAFF. Pieces in C position using the hands alternately.

Most pieces have DUET parts that may be played by the teacher, parent, or another student.

Contents

How to Sit at the Piano 4
Always Curve Your Fingers! 4
Fingers Have Numbers 5
Piano Tones 5
2 Black Keys 6
3 Black Keys 7
LEFT HAND PLAYING (♩, Bar Line, Measure) 8
RIGHT HAND PLAYING (Double Bar) 9
SING ALONG! (♩) 10
END OF SONG! 11
MERRILY WE ROLL ALONG 12
O'ER THE DEEP BLUE SEA (𝅝) 13
HAND-BELLS for Left Hand (*p*, *f*) 14
HAND-BELLS for Right Hand (Repeat Sign) 15
A B C D E F G 16
An Easy Way to Find Any White Key 17
A MELLOW MELODY (A B C) 18
A HAPPY MELODY (C D E) 19
COME AND PLAY! (Middle C Position) 20
TONGUE-TWISTER 21
MY CLEVER PUP (G–F, 4/4) 22
KITTY CAT 23
ROLLER COASTER (F–G) 24
THE ZOO (*mf*) 25
A New Position—C POSITION 26
FOR MY TEACHER 27
SAILING (♩., 3/4) 28
WISHING WELL 30
The Staff (Line Notes—Space Notes) 31
The Bass Clef Sign 32
RAIN, RAIN! 33
MRS. MURPHY'S HOUSE 34
LOOK AT ME! 35
The Treble Clef Sign 36
A HAPPY SONG 37
GEE, WE'RE GLAD! 38
LITTLE BIRD 39
The Grand Staff 40
C Position on the Grand Staff 41
MORNING PRAYER 42
A FUNNY, SUNNY DAY (Stem Direction) 43
COUNT VASCO DA GAMA 44
WHAT A SONG! 45
GRADUATION SONG 46

How to Sit at the Piano

SIT TALL!

Lean slightly forward.

Arms hang loosely from shoulders.

Elbows a little higher than keys.

Bench facing piano squarely.

Knees slightly under keyboard.

Feet flat on floor if possible. Right foot may be slightly forward.

You may place a book or stool under your feet if they do not reach the floor!

SIT HIGH ENOUGH!

If you do not have a piano stool that moves up and down, you may need to use a book or a cushion to have the correct position!

Always Curve Your Fingers!

Straight fingers have different lengths!

Curved fingers can have the same lengths!

Pretend you have a bubble in your hand. Hold the bubble gently, so it doesn't break!

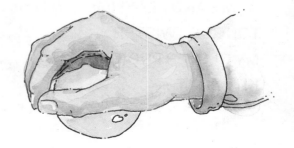

You are now ready to begin Prep THEORY BOOK, Level A.

Fingers Have Numbers

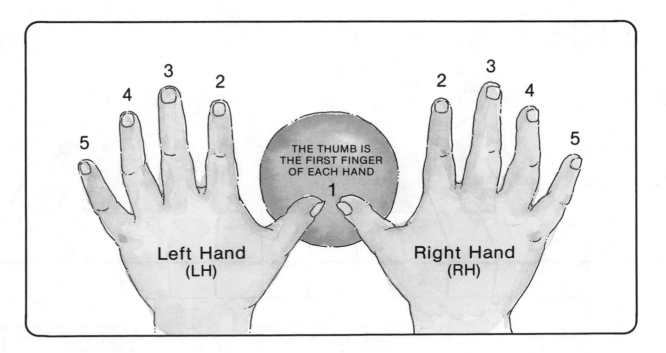

THE THUMB IS THE FIRST FINGER OF EACH HAND

Left Hand (LH)

Right Hand (RH)

1. Your teacher will draw an outline of your hands on the inside cover of this book.
2. Number each finger of the outline.

3. Hold up both hands with wrists floppy.

- Wiggle both 1's.
- Wiggle both 2's.
- Wiggle both 3's.
- Wiggle both 4's.
- Wiggle both 5's.

Your teacher will call out some fingers for you to wiggle.

Piano Tones

When you drop into the key with a LITTLE weight, you make a SOFT tone.

When you use MORE weight, you make a LOUDER tone.

For the first pieces in this book, play with a MODERATELY LOUD tone.

You are now ready to begin Prep ACTIVITY & EAR TRAINING BOOK, Level A.

2 Black Keys

2
DOWN LOW

2
IN THE MIDDLE

2
UP HIGH

DOWN (Low Notes)

UP (High Notes)

LH

3 2

1. With LH 2 3, play 2 black keys DOWN LOW (both keys at once and then one at a time).

2. With RH 2 3, play 2 black keys UP HIGH (both keys at once and then one at a time).

RH

2 3

TEACHER: The student may now play ALL the **2** black key groups,

    a) beginning with LH 2 3 on the MIDDLE group, and going ⟨DOWN⟩ the keyboard.

    b) beginning with RH 2 3 on the MIDDLE group, and going ⟨UP⟩ the keyboard.

3 Black Keys

3
DOWN LOW

3
UP HIGH

DOWN (Low Notes)

UP (High Notes)

LH

4 3 2

1. With LH 2 3 4, play 3 black keys DOWN LOW (all 3 keys at once and then one at a time).

2. With RH 2 3 4, play 3 black keys UP HIGH (all 3 keys at once and then one at a time).

RH

2 3 4

TEACHER: The student may now play ALL the **3** black key groups,

a) beginning with LH 2 3 4 below the MIDDLE of the keyboard, and going DOWN the keyboard.

b) beginning with RH 2 3 4 above the MIDDLE of the keyboard, and going UP the keyboard.

Music is made up of **short** tones and **long** tones. We write these tones in **notes,** and we measure their lengths by **counting.**

BAR LINES divide the music into equal **MEASURES.**

QUARTER NOTE
a **short** note.

COUNT: "One"
OR: "Quarter"

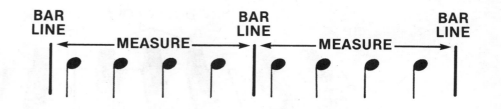

BAR LINE ← MEASURE → BAR LINE ← MEASURE → BAR LINE

LEFT HAND POSITION

LH

3 2 MIDDLE

Left Hand Playing

1. Clap (or tap) ONCE for each note, counting aloud.
2. Play & say the finger numbers.
3. Play & sing the words.

(Note-stems DOWN for LH notes)

LH Fingers:

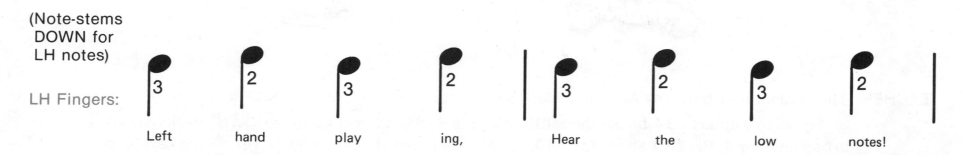

3	2	3	2	3	2	3	2
Left	hand	play	ing,	Hear	the	low	notes!

You are now ready to begin Prep FLASH CARDS, Level A.

RIGHT HAND POSITION

Right Hand Playing

1. Clap (or tap) the rhythm, counting aloud.
2. Play & say the finger numbers.
3. Play & sing the words.

DOUBLE BAR — used at the end.

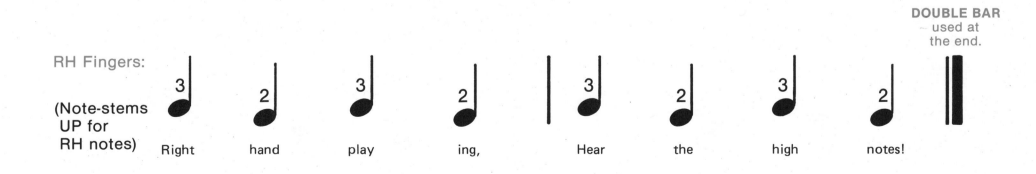

RH Fingers:

(Note-stems UP for RH notes)

3	2	3	2	3	2	3	2
Right	hand	play	ing,	Hear	the	high	notes!

IMPORTANT! *"LEFT HAND PLAYING"* and *"RIGHT HAND PLAYING"* combine to make one complete piece. Play the music on pages 8 & 9 as one song. Count aloud.

HALF NOTE
a **long** note.

COUNT: "One - two"
OR: "Half - note"

LEFT HAND POSITION

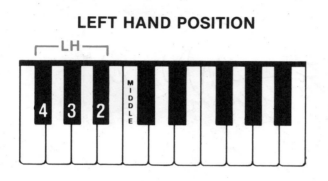

Sing Along!

1. Clap (or tap) the rhythm, counting aloud.
2. Play & say the finger numbers.
3. Play & sing the words.

LH Fingers:

2   3   4   4   3   2

Left   hand   plays;   Sing   a   long!

RIGHT HAND POSITION

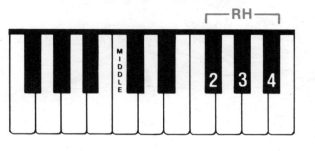

End of Song!

1. Follow 1–3 on page 10.

RH Fingers:

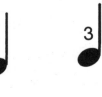

2	3	4		4	3	2	
Right	hand	plays;		End	of	song!	

2. Play the music on pages 10 & 11 as one song.
3. Play & sing the words.

12

1. Clap (or tap) & count.
2. Play & count.
3. Play & say the finger numbers.
4. Play & sing the words.

LEFT HAND POSITION

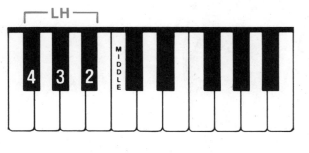

Merrily We Roll Along

(FOR LEFT HAND)

LH Fingers: 2 3 4 3 | 2 2 2 | 3 3 3 | 2 2 2 |

Mer - ri - ly   we   roll   a - long,   roll   a - long,   roll   a - long,

DUET PART (Student uses black key groups ABOVE the middle of the keyboard.)

THIS PAGE:

NEXT PAGE:

You are now ready to begin Prep CHRISTMAS JOY, Level A.

WHOLE NOTE
a **very long** note.

COUNT: "One - two - three - four"
OR: "Whole-note - hold - down"

1. Follow 1–4 on page 12.

O'er the Deep Blue Sea
(FOR RIGHT HAND)

RIGHT HAND POSITION

RH Fingers:

| 4 | 3 | 2 | 3 | 4 | 4 | 4 | 3 | 3 | 4 | 3 | 2 |

Mer - ri - ly we roll a - long, O'er the deep blue sea!

2. Play the music on pages 12 & 13 as one song.
3. Play a duet with your teacher. Use black key groups **ABOVE** the middle of the keyboard.

Hand-Bells

PART 1 (FOR LEFT HAND)

1. Clap (or tap) & count.
2. Play & count.

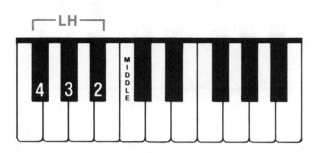

> **DYNAMIC SIGNS** tell us how LOUD or SOFT to play.
> *p* (PIANO) = *SOFT*   *f* (FORTE) = *LOUD*

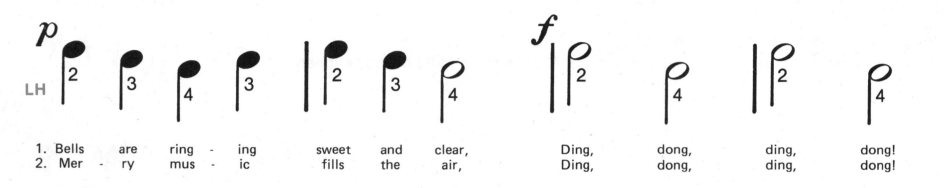

1. Bells are ring - ing sweet and clear, Ding, dong, ding, dong!
2. Mer - ry mus - ic fills the air, Ding, dong, ding, dong!

You are now ready to begin Prep SOLO BOOK, Level A.

Hand-Bells

PART 2 (FOR RIGHT HAND)

1. Clap (or tap) & count.
2. Play & count.

TWO DOTS mean go back to the beginning (on page 14) and play again.

| Hap | - py | sounds | for | all | to | hear, | Ding, | dong, | ding! |

Joy - ful sounds are ev - 'ry - where. Ding, dong, ding!

3. Play & sing the words to the whole song, beginning on page 14.
4. Play a duet with your teacher.

DUET PART

A B C D E F G

Piano keys are named for the first seven letters of the alphabet, beginning with **A.**

To find A on the keyboard: Find any 3 black key group. Play the white key between the 2nd and 3rd black keys.

1. Look at the A's on this keyboard:

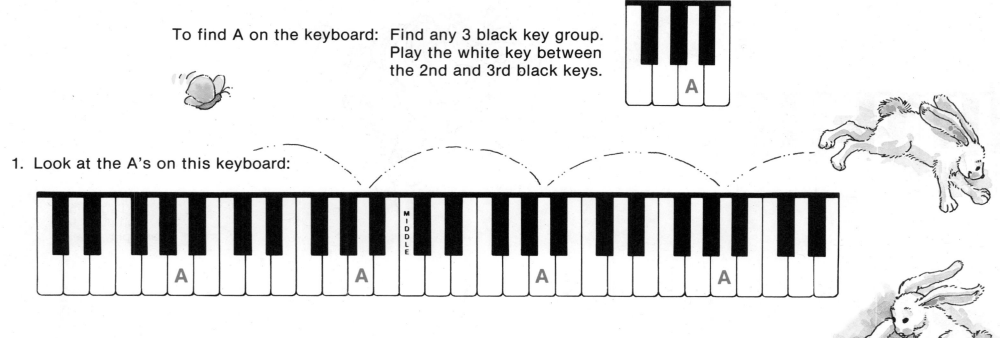

2. Find all the A's on the short keyboards below. Print an A on each one:

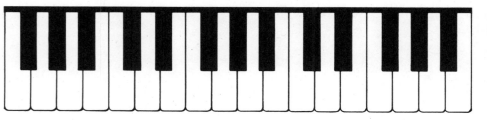

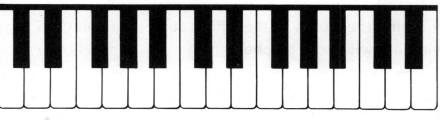

The lowest key on a full size piano is A.

You are now ready to begin Prep NOTESPELLER, Level A.

An Easy Way to Find any White Key

Play and name each of the following white keys. Play all the A's on your piano, then all the B's, etc.
Use LH 3 for keys below the middle of the keyboard. Use RH 3 for keys above the middle of the keyboard.

You can now name every white key on the piano. The key names are: A B C D E F G used over and over!

Play and name every white key going up the keyboard, beginning with bottom key A.

18

1. Clap (or tap) & count.
2. Play & count.
3. Play & say the note names.
4. Play & sing the words.

Follow these steps for each new piece.

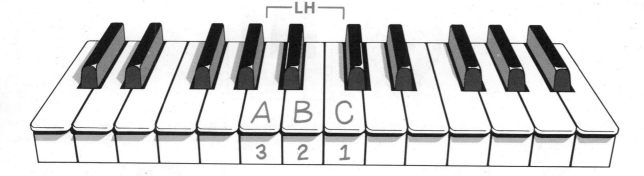

A Mellow Melody

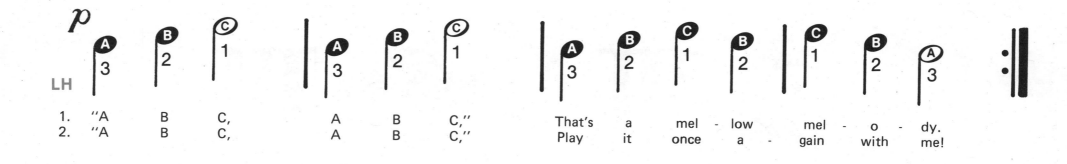

1.	"A	B	C,		A	B	C,"	That's	a	mel - low	mel - o - dy.
2.	"A	B	C,		A	B	C,"	Play	it	once a -	gain with me!

DUET PART

You are now ready to begin
Prep TECHNIC BOOK, Level A.

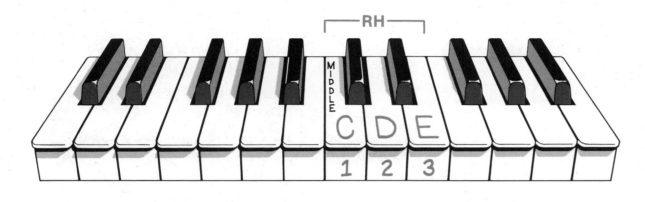

A Happy Melody

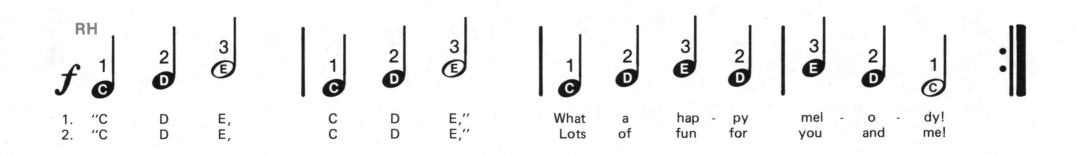

RH
f
1 C 2 D 3 E   1 C 2 D 3 E   1 C 2 D 3 E 2 D 3 E 2 D 1 C

1. "C D E,   C D E," What a hap-py mel-o-dy!
2. "C D E,   C D E," Lots of fun for you and me!

DUET PART

MIDDLE C POSITION

Come and Play!

RH = Notes with stems UP

1. Come and play! Come and play!
2. Come and play! Come and play!

LH = Notes with stems DOWN

Let the game be gin!
Try your best to win!

DUET PART

Tongue-Twister

MIDDLE C POSITION

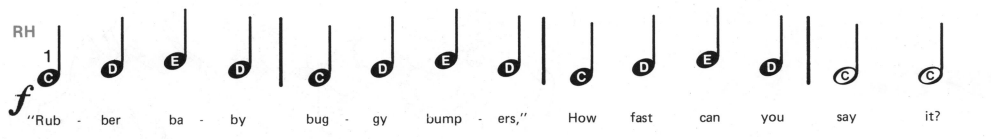

RH
1
f
C D E D C D E D C D E D C C

"Rub - ber ba - by bug - gy bump - ers," How fast can you say it?

C B A B C B A B C B A B C C
1
LH

"Rub - ber ba - by bug - gy bump - ers," How fast can you play it?

DUET PART (Student plays 1 octave higher.)

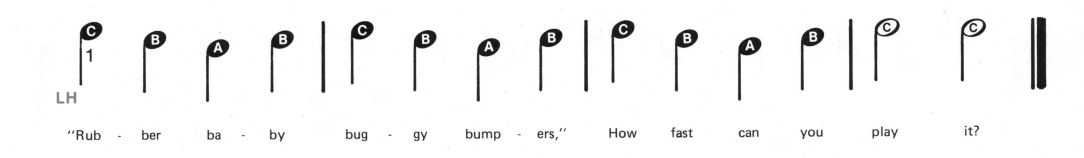

(with a bounce)

MIDDLE C POSITION

BOTH THUMBS on MIDDLE C

Music has numbers at the beginning called the **TIME SIGNATURE**.

$\frac{4}{4}$ means **4** beats to each measure.
a **quarter note** ♩ gets one beat.

My Clever Pup

RH
$\frac{4}{4}$ *f*
C(1) D E(♩) — D E(♩) F(4)

LH
C(1) B A G(4) — A B C

1. My dog's fun! My dog's neat! He's a ver - y clev - er pup!
2. He stands on his front feet, When I hold his hind legs up!

DUET PART (Student plays 1 octave higher.)

RH *(bark)*
LH *mp*

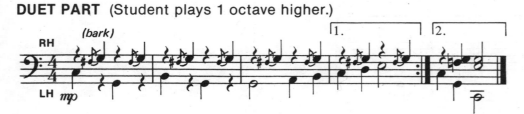

Kitty Cat

MIDDLE C POSITION

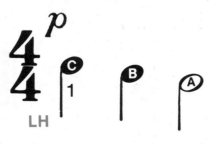
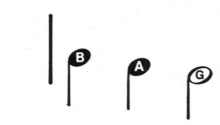
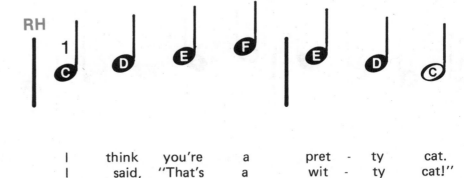

1. Kit - ty   cat!   Kit - ty   cat!   I   think   you're   a   pret - ty   cat.
2. When   you   sat   in   Dad's   hat,   I   said,   "That's   a   wit - ty   cat!"

DUET PART

MIDDLE C POSITION

BOTH THUMBS on MIDDLE C

Roller Coaster

1. Up the keys to G, and then 'way down I go to F and back to C!
2. Like a roll - er coast - er I zoom down, and then I zoom back up, you see!

DUET PART (Student plays 1 octave higher.)

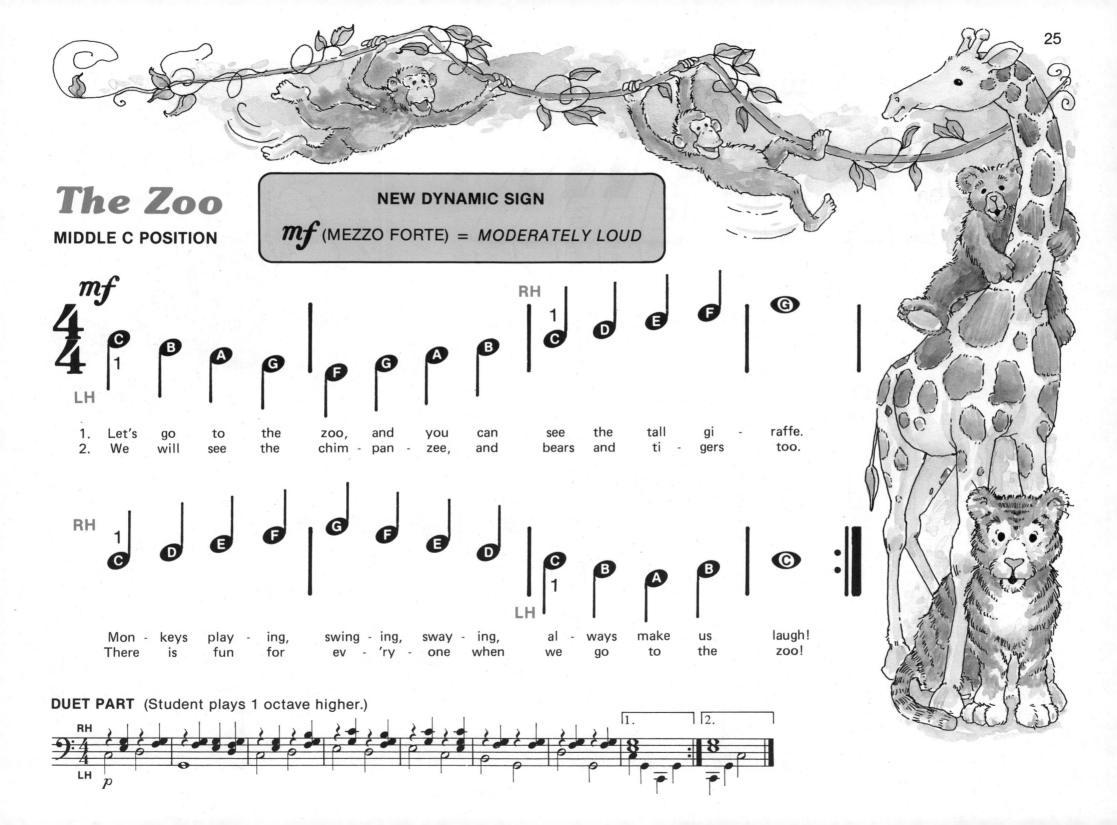

A New Position

C Position

For My Teacher!

C POSITION

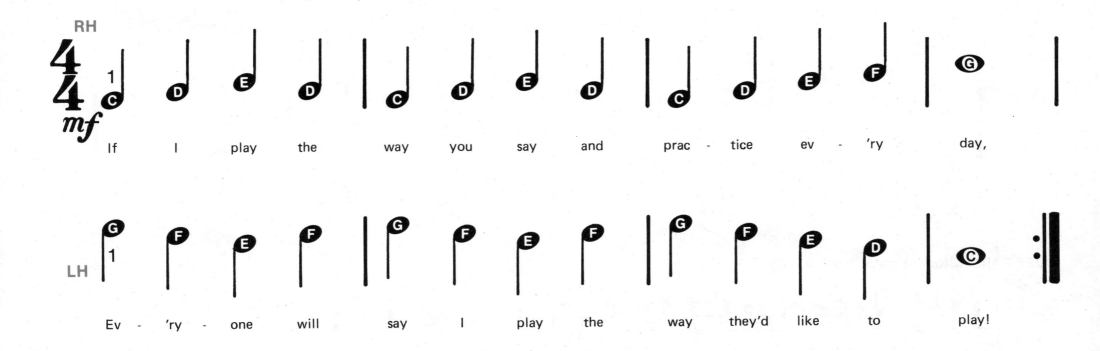

RH

4/4 *mf* 1 C — D — E — D — | C — D — E — D — | C — D — E — F — | G — | —

If I play the way you say and prac - tice ev - 'ry day,

LH

G 1 — F — E — F — | G — F — E — F — | G — F — E — D — | C — | ﹕

Ev - 'ry - one will say I play the way they'd like to play!

A NEW TIME SIGNATURE

3/4 means **3** beats to each measure.
a **quarter note** gets one beat.

DOTTED HALF NOTE
a **longer** note.

♩.

COUNT: "1 - 2 - 3"

C POSITION

Sailing

1. Come,   come,   come   to   the   sea!
2. Sea -   gulls   'round   us   will   play.

DUET PART (Student plays 1 octave higher.)

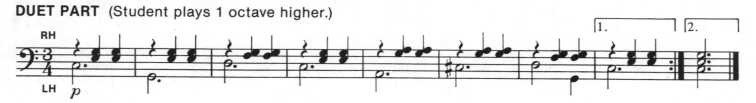

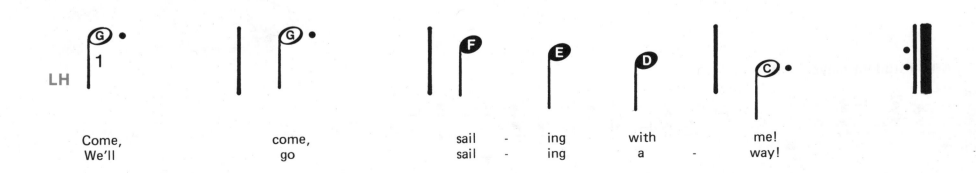

LH

Come,   come,   sail - ing   with   me!
We'll   go   sail - ing   a - way!

Wishing Well

C POSITION

Be sure to clap the rhythm before you play.

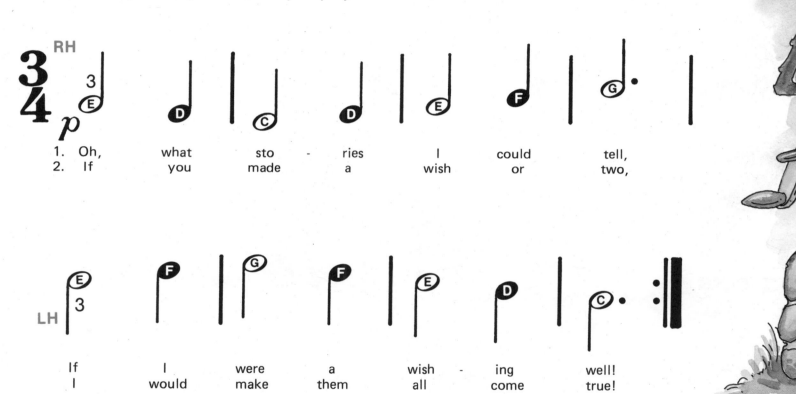

1. Oh, what sto - ries I could tell,
2. If you made a wish or two,

If I were a wish - ing well!
I would make them all come true!

DUET PART (Student plays 1 octave higher.)

The Staff

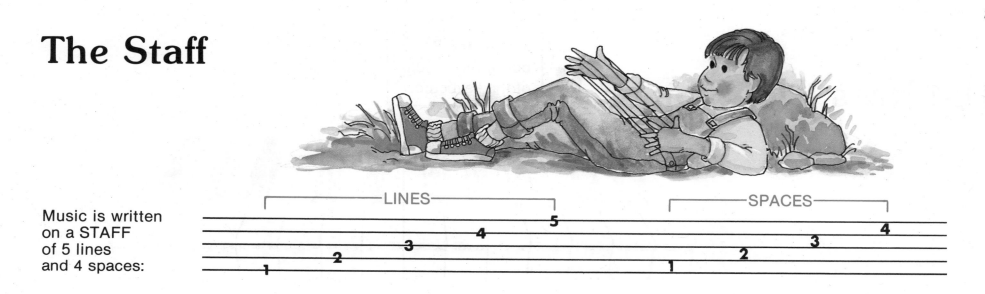

Music is written on a STAFF of 5 lines and 4 spaces:

Some notes are written on LINES:

Some notes are written in SPACES:

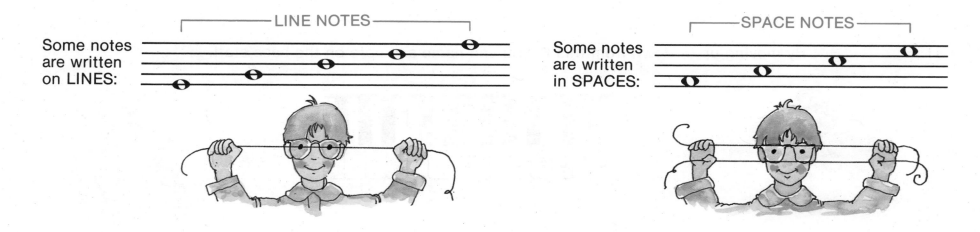

In the boxes below this staff, print an **L** below each LINE NOTE and an **S** below each SPACE NOTE.

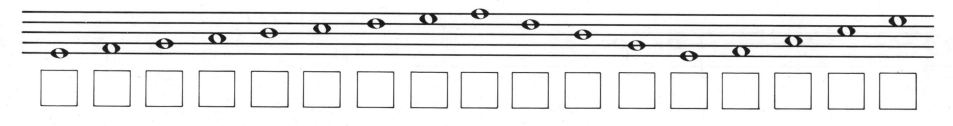

The Bass Clef Sign

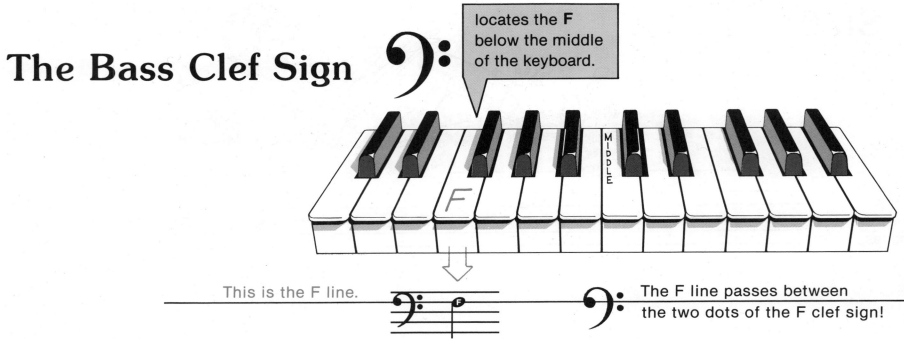

locates the **F** below the middle of the keyboard.

This is the F line.

The F line passes between the two dots of the F clef sign!

By moving up or down from this F, you can name any note on the bass staff.

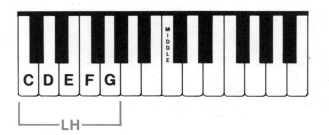

C D E F G

LH

REPEATED Notes   Notes stepping DOWN   Notes stepping UP

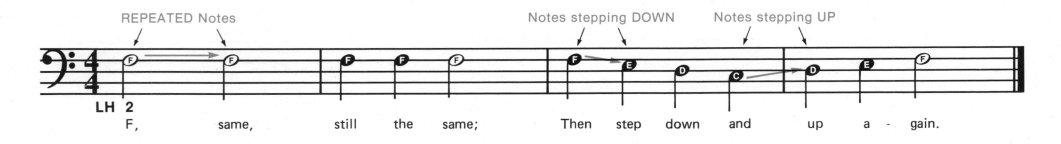

LH 2

F,   same,   still   the   same;   Then   step   down   and   up   a - gain.

Rain, Rain!

mf

LH 2

Rain, rain, go a - way! Come a - gain a - noth - er day!

2

Rain, rain, go a - way! My friend, _____ wants to play!
(add name)

DUET PART

p

Mrs. Murphy's House

f

LH 2

Dear old Mis - sus Mur - phy's house was six - teen sto - ries high, Oh!

2

Ev - 'ry sto - ry in that house was filled with ap - ple pie, Oh!

DUET PART

RH

mf LH

Look at Me!

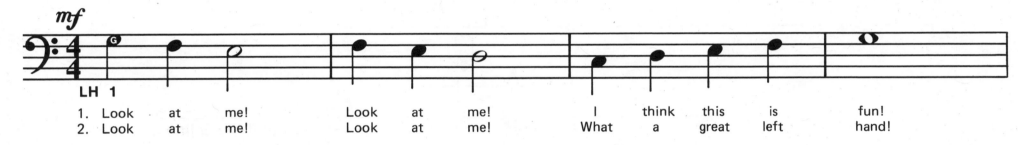

1. Look at me! Look at me! I think this is fun!
2. Look at me! Look at me! What a great left hand!

Some folks need two hands to play, but watch me use just one!
Look at me and you'll a - gree it's real - ly some - thing grand!

DUET PART (Student plays 1 octave higher.)

The Treble Clef Sign

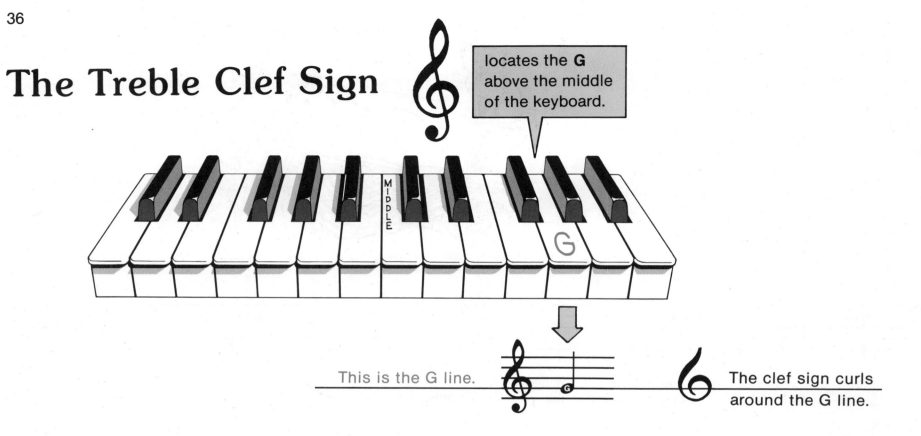

locates the **G** above the middle of the keyboard.

MIDDLE

G

This is the G line.

The clef sign curls around the G line.

By moving up or down from this G, you can name any note on the treble staff.

MIDDLE

C D E F G

RH

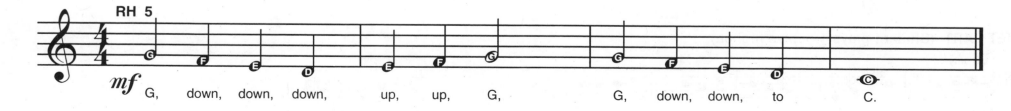

RH 5

mf

G,   down,   down,   down,   up,   up,   G,   G,   down,   down,   to   C.

A Happy Song

RH 5

f Here's a ver - y hap - py song! Play and sing a - long!

When you're sad it makes you glad to play this hap - py song!

DUET PART

mf   simile

Gee, We're Glad!

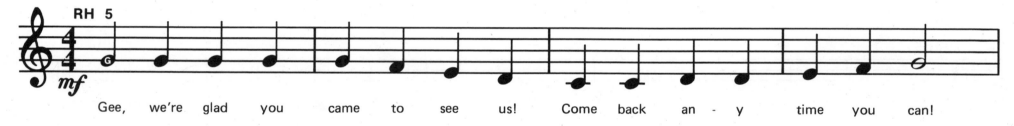

Gee, we're glad you came to see us! Come back an - y time you can!

Gee, we love to have you vis - it! Please come back a - gain!

DUET PART

Little Bird

RH 1

1. Lit - tle bird, lit - tle bird, high up in the tree!
2. Lit - tle bird, lit - tle bird, please don't fly a - way!

5

Lit - tle bird, lit - tle bird, sing your song for me!
Lit - tle bird, lit - tle bird, sing your song and stay!

DUET PART

(tweet, tweet, tweet)

8va segue

RH

LH

The Grand Staff

The BASS STAFF and TREBLE STAFF together make the GRAND STAFF.
A short line is used in between them for MIDDLE C.

The TREBLE and BASS staffs are joined together with a BRACE:

IMPORTANT! Only LH & RH **C D E F G** need be learned now!

C Position on the Grand Staff

"Position C"

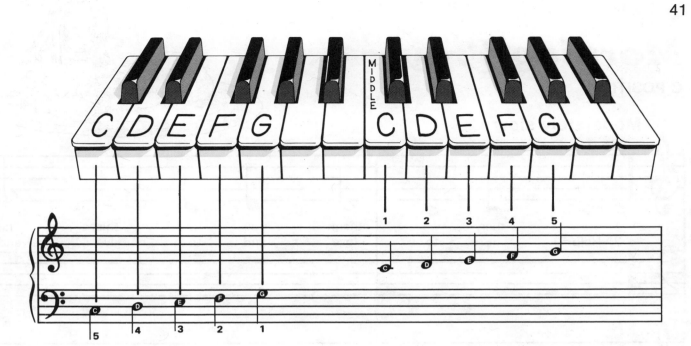

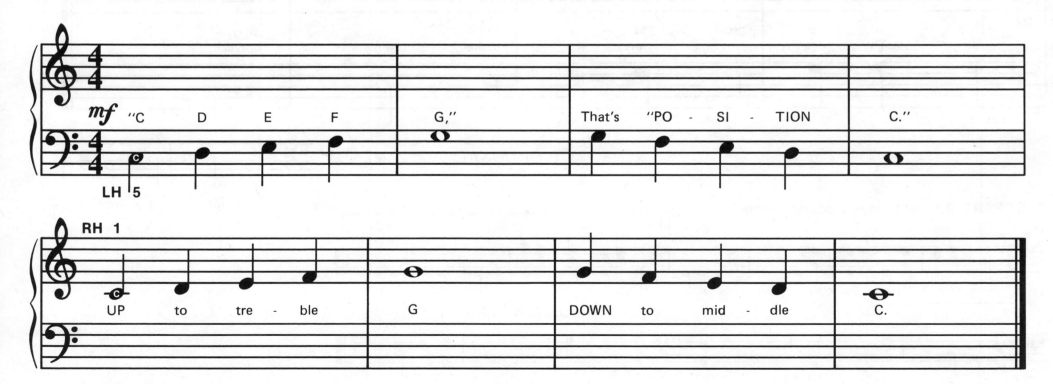

mf "C D E F G," That's "PO - SI - TION C."

LH 5

RH 1

UP to tre - ble G DOWN to mid - dle C.

Morning Prayer

C POSITION

Moderately slow

RH 1

p

1. Fa - ther, we thank you for this fine day.
2. Help us to love and give and share.

Help us to grow as we work and play.
In Thy dear name now we make our prayer!

LH 1

OPTIONAL: Add "AMENS."

2
A - men, a - men.

DUET PART (Student plays 1 octave higher.)

RH *p*

1.

LH

2.

Optional ending:

A - men, a - men.

A - men, a - men.

FOR THE REST OF THIS BOOK, Notes ABOVE or ON the middle line have stems pointing DOWN.

Notes BELOW the middle line have stems pointing UP.

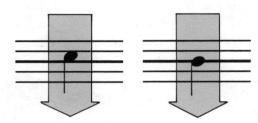

A Funny, Sunny Day

Brightly

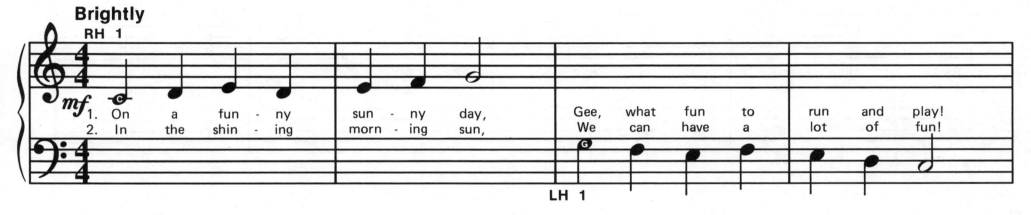

DUET PART

Count Vasco da Gama

Moderately fast

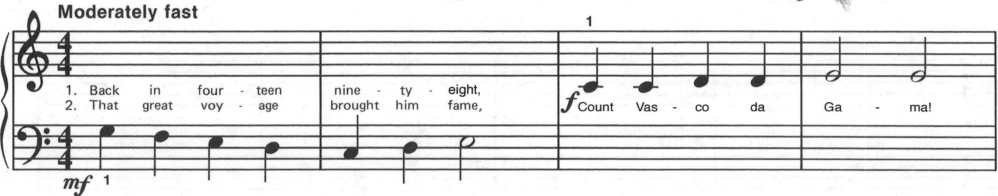

1. Back in four - teen nine - ty - eight,
2. That great voy - age brought him fame,

mf 1

1

f Count Vas - co da Ga - ma!

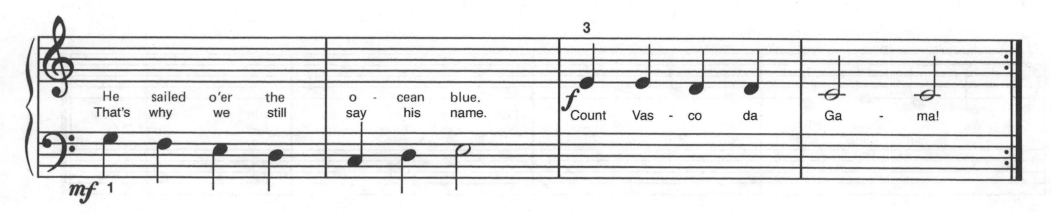

He sailed o'er the o - cean blue.
That's why we still say his name.

mf 1

3

f Count Vas - co da Ga - ma!

DUET PART (Student plays 1 octave higher.)

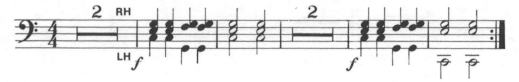

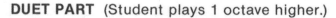

What a Song!

Happily

DUET PART (Student plays 2 octaves higher than written.)

Graduation Song

Happily

This is a ver - y im - por - tant date.

This is the day that I grad - u - ate!

DUET PART (Student plays 1 octave higher.)

This is a day I will cel - e - brate!

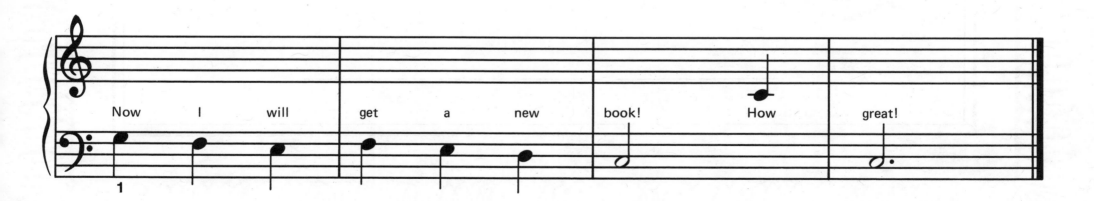

Now I will get a new book! How great!

Certificate of Promotion

This Certifies that

_____

has successfully completed
Prep Course Level A
and is hereby promoted to
Prep Course Level B.

BASIC
ALFRED'S
PIANO LIBRARY

_____ - _____
Date   Teacher